BETTER DAYS, WORSE DAYS

*Supporting a Depressed Partner
Without Losing Your Light*

DOKI COHEN

Producer & International Distributor
eBookPro Publishing
www.ebook-pro.com

Better Days, Worse Days
Doki Cohen

Copyright © 2022 Doki Cohen

All rights reserved; No parts of this book may be reproduced or transmitted in any form or by any means, electronic or mechanical, including photocopying, recording, taping, or by any information retrieval system, without the permission, in writing, of the author.

Translation: Rivkah Ben Israel

Contact: droracohen0748@yahoo.com
ISBN 9798425088604

*To my dear parents, Bilha and Eliezer Meirovitch,
may their memories be blessed.
Your absence is deeply felt.
I miss you both so much.*

CONTENTS

Why I Wrote this Book and a Little about Us 7
So, What is Depression? 13
Ways of Coping 29
Life Roles 57
Insights and Thoughts after Reading "Boker Tov
Alz eimer" by Amnon Shamosh 67
Daily Life – A Travelogue 73
Good Days, Less Good Days, and Bad Days 75
Appendix 1: Treatments that Adam Received
During his Depression 101
Appendix 2: Recommended Tools for Self-Awareness 109
Appendix 3: The Connection between the Two Books 115
Bibliography 119

WHY I WROTE THIS BOOK AND A LITTLE ABOUT US

I decided to write this book because Adam, my dear husband, has been coping with depression for over 30 years.

We will soon be celebrating fifty years of marriage. During the first 30 years of being together he was depressed. Later on, for the next 15 years we enjoyed a happy depression-free life. But, two years ago, Adam had a stroke, which , pushed him again deep into a depressive state. One that comes and goes.

I was twenty-two, and Adam was twenty-six when we got married. He had a successful insurance agency, and I worked as a programmer, analyzing systems and managing projects. During that time, I also studied parent training, a subject very close to my heart. In time, I formed parent training groups which I taught. Over the years, I acquired different therapeutic methods (Gestalt, The Work of Byron Katie, Focusing, EFT Tapping, and The Compass Method) which I applied in my work with my groups and with myself.

About a year ago, I wrote and published a book called "An Equally Worthy Child". The book deals with emotions of children's unworthiness, which as a child I had experienced, and how those feelings gradually faded away when I applied those methods to myself. At the time, I wished to share the insights that helped me get rid of those hindering feelings, so common among children and adults.

Here, too, I wish to share my experiences with those who are going through similar experiences- supporting a partner who copes with depression or any other challenging illness.

Here is my story

The first time Adam experienced depression was when he was in his forties. At that time, we both had well-paying jobs that allowed us to live comfortably. At some point, I felt I needed a change and decided to leave my job and take a break for a while. I knew that we would be able to manage financially with Adam's income. He supported my wish to take a break, yet was alarmed when I actually decided to do so.

As we no longer had the security my income provided, Adam became very frightened. His fear was so intense that he was unable to continue working at the same pace as before. That was the beginning of his anxiety cycle which in turn caused his work level to deteriorate, and consequently led to a lower income.

This trying period caused tension between us, and it was

only after starting therapy that we realized that he was suffering from depression.

During the first years when he was depressed, we went through a particularly hard time because we did not know a lot about depression, and lacked the tools to deal with it. At that time, I considered separating from Adam, but I soon realized that despite the hardships, I will continue to stick by him my only partner for life. His illness opened the way for me to understand many things about him, which were human and touching, even if they sometimes annoyed me.

Adam grew up in a poor family. He remembered those times as being especially difficult for his father, who so dearly wished to give his children everything they needed, but could not.

Being a father and husband, it was therefore, majorly important to him to provide his children with all they wanted and needed, sacrificing his own for their sake. But then, suddenly, with me quitting my job and him sinking into depression he found that his ability to fulfil that wish was compromised. .

To help supporting our household, I took a course in data security, through the employment bureau. I started to work which helped with our financial situation. But it did not allay his fears, and the depression continued.

Once we understood that this is not going to disappear so quickly, we started therapy. The psychiatrist treated Adam for many years to come, through his recurring bouts of depression, with medication and therapy.

As time passed Adam overcame the first bout of depression

thanks to the medication or my steady income and maybe both.

Throughout the years, Adam went through many periods of depression, usually due to his stopping his medication.

Many people suffering from depression stop taking their medication when they feel better, trying to eliminate its side effects. They usually stop taking their medication without letting close family members and doctors know. When the depression returns and the reason becomes clear, their partner often experiences anger not letting him know. . This was what happened to me.

We had two types of routine. The regular routine and the depressive episodes routine. Understandably, the transition from the depressive episodes routine to the regular routine was easier than the transition in the opposite direction. One of the prominent differences between the two types was the financial situation, which worsened during the times of depression. Adam would make less money and as he was in charge of the family finances these periods affected all of us. We would make an effort to tighten the belt. In a way, this was a blessing in disguise because we learned to make do with less. We were more humble and less competitive which in turn positively impacted our parenting because of its educational aspect. It also caused thoughtfulness and consideration in all of us. We kept the serious details of the situation from the children and tried to present the information in a way that suited their age. They were still aware of what was going on, and showed a lot of consideration, wanting to help and make their father happy.

A little about us as a family: we have three children and eight grandchildren. Our children do not live close by, but we are very close and receive a lot of support from them.

Adam is, by nature, a happy, good-hearted person despite the occasional depressive episodes. He raised our children very lovingly and supported them, and I am happy that today he receives a lot of support and love in return.

SO, WHAT IS DEPRESSION?

According to the dictionary, depression is defined as, "broken spiritedness." What a definition! A person's spirit- his strongest inner part- is broken.

This is not an unfixable permanent situation, but during depression, the spirit is broken. When that happens, then everything else is broken too.

In his book *Darkness Visible*, William Styron[1] describes depression as something one cannot describe to someone else, who has not experienced it. Despite this, he describes it as follows,

> "What I had begun to discover is that, mysteriously and in ways that are totally remote from normal experience, the grey drizzle of horror induced by depression takes on the quality of physical pain. But

---

1 William Styron, *Darkness Visible: A Memoir of Madness* (New York: Random, 1990) 50.

it is not an immediately identifiable pain, like that of a broken limb. It may be more accurate to say that despair, owing to some evil trick played upon the sick brain by the inhabiting psyche, comes to resemble the diabolical discomfort of being imprisoned in a fiercely overheated room. And because no breeze stirs this cauldron, because there is no escape from the smothering confinement, it is natural that the victim begins to think ceaselessly of oblivion."

Another section from the book expresses the attempt to explain how different the experience of depression is from any other experience of pain[2]:

"…it was past four o'clock and my brain had begun to endure its familiar siege: panic and dislocation, and a sense that my thought processes were being engulfed by a toxic and unnamable tide that obliterated any enjoyable response to the living world. This is to say more specifically that instead of pleasure – certainly instead of the pleasure I should be having in this sumptuous showcase of bright genius – I was feeling in my mind a sensation close to, but indescribably different from, actual pain. This leads

---

2   William Styron, *Darkness Visible: A Memoir of Madness* (New York: Random, 1990) 16.

me to touch again on the elusive nature of such distress. That the word "indescribable" should present itself is not fortuitous, since it has to be emphasized that if the pain were readily describable most of the countless sufferers from this ancient affliction would have been able to confidently depict for their friends and loved ones (even their physicians) some of the actual dimensions of their torment, and perhaps elicit a comprehension that has been generally lacking; such incomprehension has usually been due not to a failure of sympathy but to the basic inability of healthy people to imagine a form of torment so alien to everyday experience. For myself, the pain is most closely connected to drowning or suffocation – but even these images are off the mark. William James, who battled depression for many years, gave up the search for an adequate portrayal, implying its near-impossibility when he wrote in The Varieties of Religious Experience: "It is a positive and active anguish, a sort of psychical neuralgia wholly unknown to normal life."

In his book An Unquiet Mind, Jamison Kay R write the following description[3]:

---

3   Jamison Kay R. *An Unquiet Mind* (New York: Vintage Books, 1996) 217.

"...it bleeds relationships through suspicion, lack of confidence and self-respect, the inability to enjoy life, to walk or talk or think normally, the exhaustion, the night terrors, the day terrors. There is nothing good to be said for it except that it gives you the experience of how it must be to be old, to be old and sick, to be dying; to be slow of mind; to be lacking in grace, polish and coordination; to be ugly; to have no belief in the possibilities of life, the pleasures of sex, the exquisiteness of music or the ability to make yourself and others laugh.

Others imply that they know what it is like to be depressed because they have gone through a divorce, lost a job, or broken up with someone. But these experiences carry with them feelings. Depression, instead, is flat, hollow, and unendurable. It is also tiresome. People cannot abide being around you when you are depressed. They might think that they ought to, and they might even try, but you know and they know that you are tedious beyond belief..."

How very accurate.

I asked Adam how he would describe his depression and if, when describing it, he could do so as figuratively as possible. The following is his description: "It is like living in a dark place, underground, and knowing that even if I manage to get out, the end is near. There is no light, only total darkness. And as much as they may try and persuade me that there is light above ground, I know that there is not." Alternatively, "I am in the Holocaust, knowing that the gas chambers are the next step; there is no way of escaping."

A friend of mine , who also experienced depression, described it as follows:

"Suddenly, one day, I realized that I had changed. I started experiencing negative, sad feelings disconnected from my reality. My brain focused solely on sad and hopeless situations. Nothing happy or optimistic could penetrate. I spent most of my spare time simply staring into space. I could not bring myself to do anything beyond the minimal requirements of life. I lost my appetite and, as a result, I lost twelve kilograms. It was then that I realized that the situation is not good and that I need help. The doctor suggested I do a comprehensive medical checkup, which came back fine. I also went to a psychiatrist who prescribed medication that did not help. I kept searching for the right treatment. I met many therapists, none of whom I felt connected. They did not help.

Nearly a whole year went by, with no real improvement. I spent most of my time at home, feeling like I was in a huge, dark, deep shell. There was no light on the horizon.

I did everything on automatic pilot. I did Pilates every day, and I went to work which, in a way, saved me from myself. I understood that I needed professional help."

Every person experiences sadness, emptiness, boredom, and

other uncomfortable feelings. Not everyone has depression. When I experience these kinds of feelings, I call it *the blues*. It is challenging, but it passes. Depression is not *the blues*, despite there being several types of depression. Depression can last for months, and during that time, the person feels as though he is living in darkness.

Depression may stem from difficult life circumstances, such as losing a loved one, getting divorced, losing one's job, or a financial loss. Depression as a result of one of these circumstances can seem natural, so much so, that we may find it strange if we don't feel depressed. But, nevertheless, not everyone becomes depressed no matter how difficult the situation. They find their way to cope with the event, despite the difficulty, pain and suffering.

Adam suffered the loss of his beloved mother when he was four, an age when the mother is the most significant. Perhaps his loss took its toll at a much later stage, in Adam's adult life, in the form of depression.

The cause of depression is not always clear, and cannot be traced.. This type of depression tends to reoccur. In these cases, it is believed that genetics are to blame. A chemical imbalance in the brain which is passed on.

In Adam's case, we could identify the onset of his depression started. We believed it had to do with fear of financial difficulties. That was not clearcut and in time we came to understand it also had to do with his genetics.

Yet, when Adam was not in a depressive episode, a difficult situation- such as the death of his beloved sister did not trigger depression. But ,when he was depressed, no happy occasion, such as the birth of our new grandchild was able to pull him out of it.

In addition to Adam's depression we have experienced other challenging ailments, though I can say, with total confidence, that depression is the most challenging of all. Adam was ill with cancer for some years. He went through many operations, one of which was after he fell off a ladder. He spent seven months in the hospital on the verge of having his leg amputated because of complications. Despite all of that, the strain during those times did not come close to the challenge of his depressive episodes.

The challenge lies in the fact that the depressive person appears to have no serious issues at all. He has a job, a family, he is financially ok and all in all everything seems to be normal. Despite all that, he is suffering. People around him do not always understand, and react in a way such as , "Why are you making such a big deal?" "Get a grip on yourself" "See how Jacob, who got fired, is functioning just fine," and the like.

These remarks do not help or may at most, help for a short

while. That leaves the one suffering from depression all alone, misunderstood and feeling he is "just making a fuss."

So, what characterizes depression and what are its side effects?

I will differentiate between the characteristics and the side effects of depression and will also cover the side effects that partners of people suffering from depression may experience.

A. WHAT DOES THE DEPRESSED PERSON EXPERIENCE?

The main characteristics of depression are: Intense sadness; a lack of will and desire to do anything; a lack of appetite; difficulty falling asleep; a feeling of worthlessness and hopelessness - even for someone who has experienced depression in the past and has managed to move forward.

Depression is sometimes long-term and can continue for months or even years. Quite often, the wish to die also presents itself, but apart from in extreme cases, this desire is not usually acted upon.

Other emotions when suffering from depression:

1. Shame

Almost all people who suffer from depression are ashamed of it, and therefore do not share their condition with others, or share it only with those closest to them. For some reason, even though depression has become common in recent years and many people take medication to help them, it is still an issue which is not spoken about nor shared. Whereas in other illnesses, the ill person will usually enjoy sympathy from others, interest in their well-being, in the case of depression, the person feels alone, with shame playing a big part in adding to his suffering.

Adam described his feeling of shame: "I am ashamed of myself, and I feel like I am nothing, not worthy, like a rag, as if I have a mark of Cain. Everyone can see what I am going through and lack confidence."

Shame seems to be a dominant factor in depression, which means that the person feels less worthy when compared to others. There is a direct connection between depression and a person's self-worth. I dealt with the subject of self-worth at length in my first book, "An Equally Worthy Child", which helped many people improve their feeling of self-worth.

2. Guilt

Many people who suffer from depression feel guilty of the suffering they cause to their dear ones. I asked Adam to share his thoughts about his guilt feelings. He said, "The biggest guilt I feel is about the next generation. I feel a huge amount of guilt and fear that one of my descendants will suffer from depression. I cannot deal with the thought that someone will suffer because of me."

Another source of guilt for him, although a lesser one, is the time we spend worrying and taking care of him. Investing a lot of time and money in the attempt to make his situation better. He feels he has made us stop our routine lives for him.

3. Jealousy

A person suffering from depression usually feels that everyone around them continues living their lives while his life has stopped. I asked Adam to tell me more about this feeling, and he said:

"I am jealous of everyone. I walk down the street, see people that I do not know, and think to myself, He has it easy, and even if he has it hard, he can cope. I cannot do anything. Jealousy is such an awful feeling. When friends stop by, I am happy but at the same time, I am jealous. I see how busy they are, working and traveling, whereas I am doing absolutely nothing."

4. Fear

Quite often, anxiety attacks go hand in hand with depression. When anxiety accompanies depression, it is hellish. The deep sadness of depression intensifies with anxiety and is experienced as a terrifying fear of death. Adam described it: "I felt lost, frightened and terrified. I felt that there is nothing to live for. It is so hard to feel frightened. My entire body shakes. It is quite impossible to describe the experience . It is a pain of both the soul and the body."

5. Loneliness

We are all aware of loneliness and experience it from time to time. For someone suffering from depression, loneliness is a constant experience, even when surrounded by dear ones. As Adam describes it: "I feel as if I am alone in a war. My family surrounds me and supports me all the time, but I want even more support and interest from my surroundings. I want them to ask me what is going on with me, out of genuine care for me, so that I will feel that whoever asks and shows interest, really cares.

B. WHAT DOES A DEPRESSED PERSON'S PARTNER FEEL?

I wish to describe how the depressed person's partner feels because I belong to that group. Children are usually involved in what goes on, and in how the situation is dealt with when a parent suffers from depression. However, they experience it differently than the partner (I am talking about the most recent depressive episode when our children had families of their own unlike the depressive episodes when they were still living at home).

The children worry from afar. It may even be that they worry more than the partner. That is natural But, they are busy with their own lives, whereas the partner, even when working himself has his other job, looking after his depressed partner.

The heaviest burden of taking care of a depressed person falls on his partner, – physically and emotionally. The feelings of heaviness, worry, and sorrow envelopes the entire home. Complicated and conflicting feelings are often part of the partner's feelings as well. On the one hand, worry, fear, stress, anger, sorrow, shame, blame, and sometimes-even hatred overshadow our lives. On the other, care, empathy, and compassion prompt him to support and help.

When I analyze my feelings, I realize that I panic every time Adam's depressive episode starts. I know that our daily routine is about to change and we are beginning an undefined period of a different kind of life. The more these episodes occur, the more the first kind of feelings described above lessened, and the more the second group of feelings intensified.

I panic less; I know what is about to happen; I know that the children are supportive; I know that I am capable; I know that it is temporary and that better days are on the way.

C. THE DOMINANT SIDE EFFECTS FOR PARTNERS, AS I HAVE EXPERIENCED:

1. Shame

The partner of the depressed person often experiences shame himself.

I remember that in Adam's first depressive episodes, I felt shame. Adam was not the man I had married. I found it hard when spending time with close friends, who knew about his condition. Everyone was happy and laughing, but Adam was quiet and felt uncomfortable. As for friends who were unaware of his condition, I was scared they would realize that something was amiss. I felt also ashamed thinking this might prove that we have failed as a couple, shows failure in our mutual support in times of crisis, or even that we were mismatched and he was not the partner I want to stay together with.

2. Blame

Humans are used to blame one another. When our partner is depressed, it is easy to accuse him with accusations such as: "See what you have caused us" or "It's all because of you." Our routine is cut short, and we cannot do everything we planned. Then it is easy to point an accusing finger.

3. Guilt

We are used to feeling guilty. Such is the way of the world. In times of depressive episodes, thoughts crop up, like: "Maybe it's because of me; maybe I played a role in all of this? And if it is because of me, what can I do to make it better?"

4. Anger

Anger can appear quite often; it will usually do so suddenly and without warning. I can be calm and serene when suddenly anger erupts. Angry feelings can lead to thoughts like, "You are stopping everyone's lives" or "Everyone around you works hard and worry, and, meanwhile, you are self-indulgent", and so on.

5. A Heavy Burden

There were times when I felt that the burden was too heavy for me to carry. It was so hard to bear it. At the same time, I wanted people to pay attention to me, to take an interest in me, to ask, understand me and love me.

6. Sorrow, Sadness and Pain

When someone close to us is suffering and in pain and we cannot help him, it is difficult. As a result, we experience sorrow, sadness, and pain. The longer a depressive period lasts, the harder it becomes.
I am sad that Adam suffers so much. It pains me that the children see him in this state, want to make him happy, and cannot. I am pained on my behalf too. I enjoy being happy and laughing, but I do not know whether it is better to restrain myself when Adam is suffering from depression, or to be happy and laugh next to him. It is often hard for me to be happy in his presence, then I worry that maybe this makes the situation worse and intensifies his bad feelings.

WAYS OF COPING

People suffering from depression take medication and go to therapy, but what about their partners who suffer too, and cope alone, with no help? What can make things easier for them?

I wish to write about how I coped, what helped me endure the challenging periods and sometimes even made me feel stronger. I am going to suggest ways of coping, from my personal experience, that can improve one's quality of life and could help others get through this period with more ease.

Not everything that I suggest will suit everyone. Each person should do what is right for him, but perhaps some of the ideas that I suggest will help those experiencing something similar.

Firstly, I believe that it is essential that I take care of myself so that I will have the strength to take care of Adam, just as in an emergency on a plane, a parent has to don his mask before taking care of his child. We are in a situation whereby we want to save people, our partner and ourselves. Our depressed partner is, in some ways, like a child.

Perhaps the word "save" is not the right one, because a person cannot save anyone except himself. Having said that, when our partners are experiencing depressive episodes, we provide support, and perhaps sometimes save them.

How to Cope - My Ways of Coping with the Situation

The following describes things that helped me cope with the situation.

1. Activities that are Important to Me and Help Me

It was clear that I needed to take care of my well-being by doing things that make me feel happy and do me good. As a child, I was once called egotistical, someone who worries more about herself than others, which embarrassed me. Today, I do not care what people call me. I will not give up on taking care of myself, and being the partner to someone who is depressed, it is so important.

So, what should I do?

I continued playing bridge, hardly missing a lesson. I enjoyed the learning and the socializing that these lessons provided. I continued swimming in the sea, which does me good, looking at the blue waters and swimming for forty minutes. I make sure to swim two to three times a week when the weather permits. These activities did not take a lot of time, which meant that I did not leave Adam alone for long, and I could return quickly if he needed me.

We continued going to the cinema, which we both really enjoyed. During depressive episodes, Adam did not want to go as much, but he would accede to my requests to do so.

Every few weeks, we would meet with a group of friends. I would insist that he come, even though he did not always want to. He knew that his friends understood when he was going through a depressive episode because he would not be his usual funny and active self.

When he did not wish to go , I would go by myself as I loved those get togethers.

I did not give up helping with our grandchildren. In the past two years, three were born to our three children, making up a total of eight grandchildren.

We are very close to them and so it was important for me to continue helping. Helping them helped me too, in feeling stronger every time I spent time with them.

Our children live far from us, which meant that getting there took a long time and we would stay there longer. Therefore, on days that I could leave Adam alone, I would go. At other times, I had to forego a visit, or Adam would accompany me.

2. Trips

Taking trips is something else that I enjoy doing but that came to a halt during depressive episodes. Then, it is impossible to go on long trips. However, I did not give up on them entirely, and found ways to compromise. For example, we took a three-day vacation in Crete with the children. It was close-by, cheap, and short. Honestly, Adam did not feel happy, but he did feel proud of his family. Most importantly, the children and I enjoyed ourselves, spent time together, and returned home with renewed strength and energy.

I am planning more trips, longer ones. I know that I will need to see to it that someone will be with Adam when I am away, but I am sure that it will be possible.

3. Friends

I believe that friends can help during depressive episodes but it is important not to feel embarrassed and not to behave as if everything is ok. My good friends are aware of our situation, they know that it is hard for Adam and hard for me to see him like that. I feel comfortable sharing what I am going through with the circle of friends that surrounds me.

It was important to me that Adam would stay in touch with our friends. I would invite friends around, who I knew Adam felt comfortable with, and we would talk openly about his condition. It helped Adam and me feel that we are not entirely alone, that people's hearts are open and loving, which and it gave us strength.

We are friendly, well-loved people. Despite this, during his depressive episodes, Adam and I would sometimes feel quite alone. This feeling intensified as time passed.

Another important factor is that we are relatively new in our neighborhood in Zichron Ya'akov. We lived in Jerusalem most of our years together and moved to Zichron Ya'akov to be close to our grandchildren. But we have not succeeded in making new, close friends, and now we feel this lack more than ever.

It's easier when our old friends come to visit, as then Adam has no time for his depressive thoughts that constantly run through his head. We chat, and as time goes by, I can see that it does Adam and myself good. Sometimes I feel that it is hard for him because he sees friends who continue on in life, enjoying themselves, whereas he remains stuck in his pain, and then the jealousy rises.

In difficult times, one reveals who one's true friends are, and sometimes, it can be disappointing. At a certain point, I understood that our friends are busy with their own lives and not always free to be there for us when we need them. In addition, sometimes people do not want to get too close to a depressed atmosphere because it scared them. In our case, there were very few who truly disappointed us and when it happened, we managed to let it go. I understood and they, in turn, stayed close.

I would sometimes dared to ask good friends to come. They could not always come and sometimes I was offended. When people would not visit for a while, even if I had not actually asked them to come, I would find myself keeping score and finding it hard to let it go.

I found it hard when people, who were quite close to us, would ask, "How are things?" once a month. In the beginning, I would share what was going on, but in time I made do with only short answers. I very much wanted to say, "It is hard for me to share with you because you keep disappearing, and I feel offended," but I was not brave enough to say so.

I learned another important thing, to let go of my tendency to be dramatic or miserable in those meetings. At the end of the day, when I dwelled on how miserable I was (even if I had reason to be so) the gain was short-term, and I would end up paying the price for it later on. There were issues best discussed in a more suitable setting, such as in therapy.

The depression helped me get rid of behaviors that had done me no good throughout my life. I needed to feel people's support and to know that I was not alone in being responsible for things. As I mentioned, it is difficult for friends to fulfill this need, as each one is busy with his life, and at our age, each individual's world is complicated.

4. Close Family Members

Whoever can get help from close family members should do so with open arms. Only family members can truly provide support and share the burden of responsibility. I was lucky to enjoy support from my children. They wanted to help so much. All three dearly love Adam, and they wanted to return what he had given them over the years, not because they had to but because they wanted to. The three of them had babies at the time, so the amount of substantial help they could offer was limited. What was more important was that I felt that they cared about Adam and me.

I did not share everything with them. I did not want to burden them with unnecessary things that they could not help with in any case, but they constantly asked. I could not lie that everything was fine when it was not. I found it important to hear their opinions on vital decisions, and would ask what they thought.

We have a large house with a garden, so when the children come to visit, they often stay overnight. It is not so easy but, at the same time, it is also a lot of fun. It is not easy because it requires an effort, there is a lot of noise, which is harder for Adam than in regular times. He finds the mess difficult. Additionally, he cannot give his grandchildren what he wants to most of all, himself. Even though I know that he finds it hard, I do not give up on those visits which were very important for me and despite the difficulty, it is important for Adam not to lose contact with them.

The children and their spouses help, and I feel comfortable asking for it. It is a time of togetherness. The grandchildren (eight of them) know one another and bring us much joy.

They make me happiest of all, and they awaken my endless love, which is always the best kind of medicine, especially in the case of depression. When we are loving, laughing, and busy, it's a huge help. If someone feels low, other people can console him. If we fall together, we get up together. The older grandchildren, who are aware of the situation, say simple sentences such as: "Grandpa, I love you," and the younger grandchildren hug.

Sometimes arguments and anger happen. We have learned to speak openly. We are not afraid to do so because love and care are at the core of everything. Anger and shouting are not threatening; there is no need to be frightened or hide things from one another. These are such important concepts that take years to understand and help a lot with difficult situations such as depression.

5. Coping with Difficult Emotions

As I mentioned earlier, both the depressed person and his partner can experience difficult emotions, which is vital to know how to cope with. Sometimes you have to know how to "let them live" without judging or waging an inner war. If someone supporting a depressed person ends up exhausted and experiences untreated difficult emotions, the situation becomes unbearable.

It is not realistic to think that difficult emotions will never arise. It is also unrealistic to assume that we will always know how to let them go. Our automatic reactions to others and ourselves are often judgmental. Making things worse. We should learn to observe, softly and compassionately, that which is happening to us in difficult times. Judgment is a habit that we got used to over the years that probably helped us or even saved us when we were young and dependent on grown-ups, but that which we are in less need of today. We are, however, always in need of sympathetic, soft, compassionate support for ourselves.

COPING WITH DIFFICULT EMOTIONS

Coping with Shame

When Adam experienced his first depressive episodes, I felt ashamed. Actually even before his depressive episodes I lived with shame. I write a lot about it in my first book. I had no reason to feel ashamed, no one does. In our society, many live in a state of constant shame. Parents are ashamed and they pass the shame on to their children.

What makes us feel ashamed? It could be connected to a trait, an act, our external appearance, things we have said. Many of us think, "If people only knew that…that will be the end of me."

We are often jealous of certain people's wealth, academic status, social status, and so on. If we get to know people and speak to them openly, we will discover that they too are ashamed of certain things. Few people feel good about themselves and do not experience any shame, they believe that other people know that they have shameful secrets.

When I lived with shame, I was ashamed of my partner, and of course, his depression. Shame that one projects on one's partner, and it does not matter why, hides shame of oneself.

I am happy to say that for quite a while, I am, almost entirely, unashamed of myself. If I try to identify what helped me stop feeling ashamed, I can identify several insights that I picked up throughout my life, such as:

- Understanding that I am not the only one who is ashamed
- Understanding that shame brings me the most suffering, even more than the thing that I am ashamed of
- Understanding that the shame has developed in early childhood when I was entirely dependent on my parents and needed them to fulfill basic needs. I needed them to see me, love me unconditionally and support me. I needed to be able to trust them. My parents could not fulfill all of these needs for many reasons (much like many parents at the time). As a result, I thought that I was not good/worthy enough (this is what a child usually experiences when he does not receive that which he so dearly needs), and so the feeling of shame is born.

When I matured, I learned to provide myself with these needs without the belief that I am not good/worthy enough, and, as a result, the shame disappeared. This change took place over time as I gained awareness.

Today, I know how to recognize my needs. I know how to feel them in my body, to allow them freedom of expression, and to listen to them. I also know to connect to the shame that still occasionally occurs, and to feel it in my body. Connecting to these feelings is comforting, empowering and helps them disappear. When I am ashamed of Adam's depression, I immediately check how the shame reflects back at me, in what way am I still ashamed of myself.

It seems that it is impossible to entirely free oneself from shame. This understanding eases coping with the occasionally occurring experience of shame. I tend to see it as a part of me that still needs purifying so as to uncover my truth, always softly and with compassion.

When I learned to be less ashamed, I stopped being ashamed of Adam's depression. Today I can say that I feel proud of him because despite his difficulties and his will to die he continues trying and won't give up. If that is not worth being proud of, then what is?

Here is a quote from my first book, "An Equally Worthy Child" that deals with the feeling of worthiness,

> The UN's Declaration of Human Rights (10/12/1948) announces that we are all born equally worthy, "All human beings are born free and equal in dignity and rights." The word "equal" is somewhat confusing, as we are also very different. Each one of us is unique and special, like our fingerprints – there is no other like them in the entire world. Each person has his inimitable characteristics and skills, and his distinctive line of development. Yet along with our differences and individual uniqueness, we must remember that

we are all "equally worthy." Possibly, we are different in bulk weight, but are equal on the ounce.[4]

I do not believe that anyone is less worthy, so when Adam feels less worthy when experiencing a depressive episode, I continue to appreciate him and be very proud of him.

Coping with Blame

When we started our depression journey, there were times when I would get angry with Adam and blame him. After doing so, I would withdraw and experience difficult emotions that would present themselves after the initial illusion of strength and power.

With time, I understood that I could only take responsibility for myself. I cannot take responsibility for Adam. I have to take responsibility for my actions and feelings. There is no room for blame. Blame is a way to avoid responsibility and achieve a few moments of fake strength by blaming the other. Having said this, I still occasionally blame him. I have learned to contemplate my actions without judging myself. After doing so, I check what happened to me, what it aroused in me, and sometimes even learn something new.

---

4   Doki Cohen *An Equally Worthy Child* (Israel: Focus Publishing, 2018)

Even if it is difficult for Adam to get out and enjoy himself during his depressive episodes, I can still find enjoyment. It leads to a different feeling than wretchedness, being a victim, and weakness.

I still fail at times, but the most important thing is to treat myself compassionately and softly at times of failure, rather than in a judgmental way. This is hard to do at the exact moment of failure, but it can be done afterwards, better late than never.

Coping with Guilt

I could have played a part in Adam's depression. It is always possible to think that perhaps we contributed to the situation. These thoughts are never-ending, we will never know if that is the case, so there is no point in feeling guilty. It is better to think about how we can help one another and concentrate on that. The habit of feeling guilty and blaming holds us back and stops us from developing.

Coping with Anger

I feel angry when something startles me, and then I feel powerless. I am familiar with anger from the times before Adam's depressive episodes. Then when I occasionally thought that I was angry because of him, I understood that I was not being honest with myself. Anger was always present because I chose to be angry. When Adam angers me, I know that it is something about myself, reflected through him. Then I know I should figure out what that thing is in me because Adam is simply acting as a mirror.

For example, I noticed that I get angry when Adam would panic about expenses. When I contemplated on it, I discovered that his panic would trigger my panic. I panic when our finances are taking a turn for the worse. I knew that this was an excellent opportunity to check myself and ask myself why I was afraid. I would ask myself what could be the worst thing that could happen, what this reminds me of from my past, what I gain and lose from panicking, and so forth. My discoveries can help me grow and enable me to let go of fears that are preventing me from living each moment fully. I embrace the need to overcome difficulties and grow, so I view these instances as excellent opportunities.

Coping with the Weight of Responsibility

Sometimes the burden is heavy, and it is hard to carry it alone. When there is no internal or external support system, the burden becomes unbearable.

In recent years, I needed less external support because I learned to support and forgive myself. I was not ashamed to admit that I was having a hard time, that I needed people to come, and that I wanted a hug. When you ask honestly and openly, you receives them, and even if you don't life goes on.

Coping with Pain and Sadness

We fight against the feeling of sadness, as if sadness needs to be gotten rid of as quickly as possible. Some claim that depression is the sadness that we did not allow ourselves to feel, and it grew until it became depression. Sadness is the other side of happiness. Every feeling or emotion has its counterpart:

> Hate vs. Love
> Jealousy vs. Contentment
> Sadness vs. Happiness
> Cold vs. Hot
> Loneliness vs. Belonging
> Courage vs. Fear
> Despair vs. Excitement

We want to only feel those emotions which we consider positive. I do not call emotions positive or negative because I believe opposite feelings complement one another. All emotions are human. Some are pleasant while others are not. If we want to experience pleasant emotions in their entirety, we should be willing to experience the unpleasant ones in their entirety too.

When we accept all the emotions which may arise, the pleasant ones will have their place, as well as the unpleasant ones. We will be able to experience each one authentically, and each emotion, whether pleasant or unpleasant, can contribute something to us. When one accepts the feeling of sadness, it cures us. When one does not, it weakens us.

When we allow ourselves to experience every emotion that presents itself, it will arise and then dissipate, making room for the next one. Much like when we are hungry, we eat and don't feel hungry anymore. When we do not allow ourselves to experience an emotion, it can take over, and then instead of feeling sad occasionally, we become sad people, and the difference between the two is significant.

It is vital to allow these emotions and sensations to be present.

Nowadays, many therapy methods emphasize the importance of allowing emotions to rise. Not for the lack of choice, nor because trying to fight them or deny them can perpetuate them, but rather because that which arises needs to arise, and it does so for a reason. It may be harder to allow feelings to present themselves and to accommodate them when doing so alone. It is a good idea to have someone who can support you during the process. You can learn to do so using the Focusing method, Byron Katie's "The Work" method, or other methods.

6. Sources of Support for Family Members

I discovered that there are organizations that provide support for family members of people suffering from depression, and I decided to turn to them to see what they offer. Firstly, I turned to the community Welfare Department and the social worker in our clinic. They told me about the "Mental Health Consultation & Guidance for Families" Centers that offer group and one-on-one meetings.

I decided to go to the one-on-one meetings to talk about what I was going through, lighten the emotional burden and get support without paying exorbitant amounts of money as our expenses were constantly growing. I enjoyed having the weekly opportunity to share the difficulties I was going through caused by Adam's depression, To be the focus of attention for an hour, and to get support and enjoy admiration. I needed to feel that I am an important and interesting person.

People supporting family members with depression can gain strength, support, practical advice, and social support in trying times from group meetings. Group members can help us feel understood and embraced.

7. The Search for Meaning

We need to feel that we are meaningful and to have things in our lives that are meaningful to us. It is hard to live with a feeling of emptiness, especially when living with dear ones who suffer from depression. We want and need to help them but wish to avoid plunging into feelings of emptiness and lack of meaning.

I always felt that I had meaningful things in my life, such as the work I enjoyed. I worked in computing and took part in wonderful projects together with my colleagues. I went to work feeling happy and full of anticipation. I enjoyed developing the system I was working on, or solving bugs that users had reported.

I also enjoyed my work in parent training, both my studies and working with the parents. I felt that I was doing a good job helping many parents.

When I felt emptiness and a lack of meaning, I had less strength to deal with Adam's depression and support him. I feel the need to emphasize how essential the feeling of meaning in one's life is for a person dealing with a depressed partner.

In the past six months, I experienced meaningfulness in many aspects of my life; in the love for our grandchildren; in the distribution of my book "An Equally Worthy Child" (hoping it will make a difference such as in schools and parents); in writing this book, and in helping my dear Adam.

Even in times of anger, frustration, and helplessness, one can experience meaningfulness. Finding meaning in difficult times is a lifeline in the darker times, and when they happen, it helps to get up faster.

8. Financial Independence

Financial independence is vital especially for women. Today, women need financial independence more than ever before. They need to have the ability to earn and not be financially dependent on their partners. Financial independence provides us with a sense of freedom, not being dependent on anyone, which, in turn, promotes our confidence. Financial independence allows us, as partners of people suffering from depression, to take charge of our lives.

9. Household Help

When the household chores fall on our shoulders, it is a good idea to hire help. Teenagers can help too, often happy to make some money cleaning, shopping, or even staying with the one who suffers from depression.

WHAT NOT TO DO BEING THE PARTNER OF A DEPRESSED PERSON

1. Do Not Neglect Yourself

The partner suffering from depression often becomes the focus of attention. One should learn to give oneself space, sometimes at the expense of one's partner. The partner is indeed important, maybe even most important, but one must remember that this is not always the case at any given time.

When I say that one must "give oneself space", I mean to do things that do you good during challenging times. For example I go to a café alone or with a friend, while Adam stays at home or travels to see our grandchildren and gets huge amounts of love. I return home with renewed energy after charging up and filling my drained emotional batteries.

2. Do Not Try and Cope Alone

You do not have to cope alone. Many people who live with a partner who suffers from depression are secretive about it, not wanting other people to know. It can stem from shame, worry about how it might affect the family, the children's chances of getting married, and so forth. Coping with depression is a heavy burden that is impossible to bear alone.

I am not ashamed of Adam's depression. The opposite is true, I am proud of how Adam copes bravely with this incredible challenge and of our supportive family members. Having said that, when I shared Adam's condition with other people, I was exposing Adam, and I knew that this exposure was hard for him. It sometimes made me feel that I was doing something wrong. I did that because of my need for support, not wanting to feel alone, as well as the thought that by sharing what I was going through, I could gain ideas and solutions that could make things easier for me.

3. Do Not Be Dragged into Victimhood or Misery

We sometimes, feel sorry for ourselves. Our partners' depression might have caused us to feel that way as means to get attention and pity that we would not otherwise receive. Being miserable could gain something, , but the price we pay for doing so is higher than the gain. Misery adds depression on top of the existing depression which can lead to idleness, tiredness, and a lack of willingness to take responsibility for helping our partner and ourselves. Try not to stay in a miserable frame of mind for too long.

I tended to feel miserable when I had the opportunity to do so, but I am happy to say that I managed to break free of that tendency, along with breaking free from the question of what others think of me. These changes brought on my feelings of strength and freedom.

4. Do Not Expect Daily Changes

I will admit that I was not very good at this. Every day I would check if something had improved with Adam. I would ask him almost every day, "How are you today?" Our children would also ask, "How is Dad today?" and I would update them. This daily checking was not good for either of us, but I could not stop. We were making it clear, through our questions, that we wanted the depression to end. This might have caused Adam even more stress.

5. Do Not Share Every Expense (or the like) That May Cause Your Partner's Stress

You do not need to share every expense with your partner. When I used to do so, I realized that it was making him very stressed. I do not know how to lie, but with time I decided that it was sometimes better not to tell him, or even to hide things from him that were not that important for him to know because they would make him panic.

6. Be Assertive rather than Aggressive

It is important to feel powerful, but it is equally important not to abuse this strength by turning it into aggressiveness. During depressive episodes, we are more powerful than our partners. It may be the first time that we feel this way, or we may even we enjoy it. However, we should look for ways to allow our partners to feel they too are powerful, that they can make decisions, that they are capable. Adam cares for me greatly when he is not in depressive episodes and less so when he is. I explained to him that I need to feel cared for even when he is depressed. When he sometimes manages to make me feel that way, it empowered us both a lot. Sometimes I enjoy the feeling of power, but I remind myself each time to remain humble. Learning to be humble was a huge lesson for me, which has led to a feeling of dignity.

7. Do Not Push Your Partner to Go To Therapy

When Adam is in a depressive episode, he finds it hard to spend money. He pays for necessary things such as a meeting with a doctor or psychiatrist. But there are things he does not want to pay for, then there is no point trying to get him to do so.

I would hear about a good psychologist or social worker who might provide Adam with the support he needs, so I would try to convince him to meet him, hoping it would solve our problems. But in most cases Adam did not comply. One day my Focusing teacher offered to come to our house, meet Adam and charge for the meeting only if she could help. I told Adam about her generous offer, and he was more than happy to accept. I realized then that there is no need to push. When the time is right, things start moving in the right direction.

8. Do not Give Up on the Hope that Things Can Improve

A depressed person does not believe that he will succeed in breaking free from his depression, even if he has recovered in the past. We, as their partners, should not be dragged into this way of thinking. We have to continue to believe that their condition can change.

I have to admit that there were times when it was hard for me to be optimistic in the face of Adam's depression, and to continue to believe that the long-awaited day will arrive. Despite our experience from earlier episodes, I still felt, on occasion, that Adam would never resurface.

There is no point in fighting this, and I do not really have any good advice. You can share these feelings with someone close, someone who can understand the difficulties you are facing. You can practice self-love, and most importantly, do not blame yourself.

Not criticizing ourselves is always true, especially when we experience difficult days. It is, unfortunately, our strongest tendency, looking where we are not okay. We inherited it from earlier generations.

Two questions help me not to criticize myself:

1. What kind of world do I wish to live in?
2. Who do I wish to be in this world?

I do not wish to live in a judgmental world; I have had enough of that. I used to judge others and myself, and other people judging me would affect me deeply. The good news is that we can change our habits, even if it requires effort. One cannot simply decide not to be judgmental. Being judgmental is automatic, but one should learn to examine every judgment to see if it is true (a detailed explanation can be found in the chapter "Recommended Approaches for Awareness Work" in the paragraph "The Work Method").

Some insights that I learned along the way helped me overcome this habit: The understanding that we are not born with the trait of criticism, we learn it from our surrounding and culture. Understanding that being judgmental protected us in childhood, when we were dependent on others and did not know how to ask for what we needed. Today, as an adult, I do not need this protection, and I know how to take care of my needs in other ways.

For example, when I was a child, I felt stupid. I thought that I did not understand anything. My parents did not know how to empower me or strengthen my self-belief, that I am clever and knowledgeable. The opposite was true, at every opportunity they made me feel that I did not understand. I am sure that they did it from a good place. In those days, people thought that criticism encouraged children and helped them advance, and perhaps my parents felt that they were not intelligent either. I did not enjoy that feeling, but I held onto it believing my elders. I also held onto this belief so that my parents, who I was dependent on, would not demand things from me that made me feel threatened. I preferred to avoid failure or to be laughed at.

Over the years, I grew and developed, and this belief no longer served me well. I wanted to grow and not avoid doing things because of these fears. I preferred to take chances, try and dare.

9. Do Not Hold Back being Happy Next to Your Depressed Partner

With time, I understood that it is important for me to stay true to myself which will not affect my husband badly, even if he has no desire to laugh or be happy.

LIFE ROLES

We fulfill different roles in life that change throughout the years. This chapter focuses on the roles we chose, and those we don't.

When we choose a role, we begin full of energy, desire, and willingness to deal with challenges. We are optimistic, we feel brave, and we have a good feeling about the situation.

However, there are times when roles that we do not want demand our attention, such as caring for a sick partner. Then there are several ways we can deal with these roles.

The first is to get up and leave. The second is to stay but refuse the tasks that we need to do. Refusing takes a lot of strength and cannot lead to a happy relationship. The third possibility is doing what we need to do because we do not have a choice, not refusing but rather doing everything reluctantly. The fourth option is to replace the role that we did not choose with one that we do. This option leads to caring, willingness, and even happiness, even when knowing that we will experience pain, hardship and challenges on the way. We try to continue fulfilling our role out of choice.

I wish to share a role-switching experiment that we did, in which I tried to see things as Adam, and Adam tried to see things as me. Each one described the emotions, thoughts, and feelings that arose while playing the other.

Me going through the day as Adam:

I wake up in the morning, not wanting to get out of bed. I do not want to do anything today. Not cook, meet anyone, or go out. I do not want people to ask me how I am feeling today. I have had enough of people pitying me; I have had enough of letting people down.

Despite this, I get up and do my daily tasks slowly, brush my teeth, cream my face, get dressed, and make myself a coffee. I can see that Adam is full of energy; he has many plans; I do not even want to ask him what his plans are. It is so hard for me to watch him, knowing that nothing is a problem for him. He tidies the kitchen, takes out the ingredients he plans to cook, talks on the phone and laughs. I think how easy it is for him. His soul is not heavy, he can do whatever he feels like and everything for him happens with such ease. Will this be me, one day? After all, I do know how enjoyable it can be.

During the day, my friend calls, and after she asks how I am, she tells me about an interesting project that she got that makes her both nervous and excited. I cannot bring myself to share her happiness, even though I so want her to succeed. I am so ashamed of my feelings. It is so hard to bear, oh so hard to bear.

After that, Adam wants to go out together to see a film, and I do not have the energy to see happy people or people that I know. Adam is annoyed at me because I do not want anything, and once again, I feel ungrateful, he does so much for me, and the little that I can do for him I do not do. It annoys me that things are good for him while things are so bad for me, I want him to suffer a little too.

Adam going through the day as me:

I wake up in the morning, and I see that Doki is not doing well. I can see it on her face, from her skin color, and I think that here comes another one of those days again. I wonder if I will have the strength for it. What a heavy burden I have to carry. Who can help me? With whom can I share my struggles? Should I share them with the children? It is hard enough for them.

How long will this go on? A week? A month? Half a year? She suffers so much. I love her, and it is hard for me to see her like this. She is such a happy woman when she is not depressed. How I miss that side of her. It is also hard for me, and I need to take care of myself so that she will not pull me down too. I want to get away from the house for a few weeks, but I cannot bring myself to do that to her because she needs me. It is so hard to be entirely alone in this situation.

I want to enlist the help of people who love her, but I am afraid of being a burden. I know from experience that eventually it passes, and it helps, but only for a few minutes.

This experiment helped us understand what the other one goes through. Sometimes we think that we know what the other is going through, after all, we tell one another everything. However, when we try to put ourselves in the other's place, we experience everything that the other goes through, on all levels, physically, emotionally and psychologically, even for just a few minutes. Still we cannot truly experience what the other does. For the next few hours after our experiment, I experienced a heaviness and intense sadness but was happy that Adam had the chance to experience what I go through and to understand that even as the "stronger" one of the two of us, it is difficult for me too, .

This experience drew us closer. Suddenly, we were partners who understood one another better. Still, I believe I understood Adam better than he understood me because he was stuck in his world, which was hard for him to emerge from. I had the chance to enter his world on a deeper level, and as a result, our conversations changed from focusing on advice to focusing on understanding.

Starting in childhood, we take roles upon ourselves. It starts with each child being assigned a role by the family setup he is born into. When the first child is born, all roles are available. Once the child starts to understand what is important in the family, he can choose a preferred role. The second child does not usually choose a role that is already filled. In this way, one child chooses to be "the clever child," the second to be "the helpful child," the third "the funny child," the fourth "the diligent child," and so on.

"The clever child" cannot allow himself to act silly, and the "diligent child" cannot be lazy, because roles are binding and provide the child with a sense of worth.

When we grow up, we can understand the significance of our role, it's resulting gains and losses, and are happy to let it go so we can experience other things. Many people, however, are unaware of this possibility and hold onto their role throughout their life. Others are aware of the possibility but do not want to let go of their role.

There are also other types of roles. For example, when building a family, we need to assign roles so that the family will function. These decisions should be made as a family, and change following its changing circumstances.

Some roles we do not choose but find ourselves needing to take on because, for example, our partner cannot do it. Sometimes, one partner is sick, sensitive, or in need of rest, at which point the other partner needs to be the healthy, strong and functioning one.

On occasion, Adam takes a break from life in a variety of ways. Sometimes he is sick, sometimes he falls and needs hospitalization for a few months, and other times he is depressed.

What I am writing here could raise objections: he not only suffers; you are also blaming him for taking a break and burdening you with his difficulties? I am not a behavior specialist, so what I am suggesting here may not be accurate, but it is still important for me to bring it up.

Perhaps his need for a rest is linked to his role. Adam is a very diligent person; diligence is one of his roles in life. Often, a role that we take on does not allow us to consciously choose a different one. Meaning, the option to take a vacation and a rest is not possible for someone who has taken on the role of being diligent. However, because a diligent person also needs a break, he finds a way to rest via illness or depression, which makes it impossible to complain about his uncharacteristic behavior.

I am not stating these things accusingly because even if there is a grain of truth in them, it is clear that these actions are unconscious, done automatically and not by choice.

As I was writing this book, I came across a Facebook post written by Tal Asher, who suffers from Parkinson's disease, about the role of a sick person's partner. Her post found me on a day when I was in a lot of pain. It calmed and comforted me, I decided to quote it here. I asked her for permission, and was happy that she agreed.

Tal Asher, who is sick with Parkinson's, writes about a role that is forced on a person, the role of the supporting partner of the sick person. I found many things that she wrote which support the writings here. Even though she wrote from the viewpoint of the supported partner, she accurately describes what I experience as the supporting one[5]:

> As of late, I have been thinking a lot about a sick person's environment, the people who surround him, specifically the caregiver (the professional term for such a role), the person who is closest to the patient, usually a partner or children (or G-d forbid, parents). I could not find a fitting name in Hebrew… Perhaps the correct term is "devoted caregiver"…For our purposes, I want to focus on partners who are caregivers because I think that other set-ups have different dynamics, which is another subject for another time.

---

5 Tal Asher, Facebook, 14 Jan 2021, https://www.facebook.com/photo/?fbid=10220226590869791&set=a.1426955228722 Accessed 20 Jan. 2021.

Sometimes it looks as if in this "role play" (if we can call it that), the "devoted caregiver" is the more complex and problematic of the two. If I had the choice, I am not sure I would be prepared to switch roles. I am not sure.

Seemingly, bad luck struck the one who is sick. Fate chose the one who is sick (or whatever cliché you wish to use to describe the bombshell that landed on those chosen). So what did one whose life is linked with that person do wrong? It is not really his "problem" and theoretically, if not morally (and obviously not seen as the fitting thing to do), he can pick up and leave the struck one , to deal with his own fate. However, as I said, this solution is only theoretical, and this dilemma can come up at any given moment. And do you know what? It is easy to take a stance, but it is almost impossible to escape this dilemma and come out looking "good." After all, in most cases, the "devoted caregiver" is not a professional and does not necessarily have a caregiving temperament, and suddenly, this burden is forced upon him. And it is truly a burden. There is no pretty way to put it.

This burden includes many aspects, such as fear, guilt, anger, worry and love. Maybe also frustration, disgust, rejection, and perhaps compassion and kindness. There is a lot of embarrassment, practicing acceptance and giving on both sides. It is a matter of knowing how to deal with the entire emotional upheaval, especially when negative feelings arise. Both sides find themselves in a guilt loop for even thinking certain thoughts, as well as feeling that I am not even the subject here, he is the one suffering so why am I pushing my own suffering into the picture? That is not the way it works. The difficulty is all of ours. When illness enters a home, it affects the entire house, it touches everyone differently, and each one deals with it in his or her own way. That's why I believe that the most important sentence that you can say to someone in this situation is, "Allow yourself to feel everything that you feel, you are allowed!"

One of the most important pieces of advice that I read at the beginning of my journey was that it is so important for caregivers to find external sources of support. These sources provide a safe place where one can vent, even about the thoughts and feelings that are not necessarily "acceptable" to say aloud. I remember sharing this piece of advice with my then husband, and with my mother. In order to care for someone, a person needs strength and needs to find the external sources that can provide him with those strengths.

> I feel that the "devoted caregivers" do not receive a lot of attention because they are supporting actors in the current drama, and they view themselves as such, as they focus on the complicated role that landed on them. For this reason, I believe they can gain a lot from a designated space that will allow them to be the center of attention, or to distance themselves slightly and listen to themselves, even for a short time. This is what I wish to create for whoever needs it.[6]

Tal's post touched me, as did her viewing the supporting partner as central and not as a subordinate entity. Tal described what I experience so accurately, the two sides within me that are constantly changing, that are so different from one another.

One side worries, is compassionate and giving, while the other side is angry, afraid, even hates and feels bad about himself.

Tal writes, "Allow yourself to feel everything that you feel, you are allowed." This sentence gave me strength and helped me transform the feeling of automatic self-flagellation in times when experiencing feelings that were harder to cope with. This was Tal's gift to me.

---

6   Tal Asher, Tafkedo shel haben/bat zug shel ha chola, Facebook, 14 Jan 2021, https://www.facebook.com/photo/?fbid=1022022 6590869791&set=a.1426955228722 Accessed 20 Jan. 2021.

INSIGHTS AND THOUGHTS AFTER READING "BOKER TOV ALZ HEIMER" BY AMNON SHAMOSH

I read Amnon Shamosh's book *Boker Tov Alz Heimer* [Good Morning Alzheimer's] after reading about it in an article on his coping with his wife, Hannah's Alzheimer's . I remember how excited and moved I was after reading the article. When I heard that Amnon had written a book, I ran out to buy it. I knew that the book contains insights and messages that could make my experience easier.

Amnon describes the challenging experiences that he and his wife Hannah go through every day. He also talks about how he maintains a positive feeling, and how their house has a loving atmosphere. He talks about the advantages of the illness for their lives. He created a wonderful kind of "patent" by inventing a being called Alz Heimer on which he vents all his anger and helplessness. He claimed that not Hannah was creating the problems but Alz Heimer.

Every line in that book moved me. Shamosh's book deals with Alzheimer's, not depression, and there are, of course, differences between the two diseases. However, his insights about coping with the situation helped me. In both our cases, we learn to live with a sick partner in a way that is far from simple or standard. Both illnesses are chronic, incurable, or require a long time to recover, and so one needs to learn to live with them.

What insights did I learn from the book?

1. The importance of speaking to one's sick partner about things we did together in better times. This can do one's partner good in his difficult times. Good memories have the power to heal. They bring on laughter, moving conversations and help the time pass enjoyably. We can talk about good memories to help make plans for when better days come.
2. Despite the difficulty and fatigue, one can live life to the fullest and continue doing things that one was used to doing in the past.
3. Focus on what I gain by caring for my partner, instead of concentrating on what I am losing, such as developing tolerance, compassion for him and myself, love for him and myself and so on.
4. Difficult times can help us develop, grow, build awareness, and choose anew all that is truly important. We can choose how to react, how to accept difficult situations, and how to accept others and ourselves in difficult situations.

Shamosh shares the many things that he does on behalf of Hannah, even when it is uncomfortable and difficult for him to do, and even though there is a caregiver, whose job it is to do those things. Hannah needs him, so he steps up.

He does not view his actions as bringing him any development or growth. He describes his experience as falling in love with Hannah all over again, she who has lived with this illness for many years. Maybe it is still a kind of development and growth on his part.

If one chooses to focus on growth and development, I believe there will be fewer moments of despair. There are still difficult moments, but one can choose to accept the reality and one's reaction, instead of falling back on automatic ones. It is not the difficult moments that are important, but how we choose to relate to them. We can choose to grow via the opportunities for growth that present themselves to us, via the lessons that we experience in life.

5. Sometimes, we find ourselves in situations where we need to step aside and focus entirely on the other person. In the previous chapter, I claimed that in order to have the strength to take care of one's partner one should take care of oneself first, and only then focus on one's partner. Shamosh claims that there are situations when we need to take care of our partners while stepping aside.

Despite Shamosh suffering from a serious problem himself (he is blind in both eyes) and needing support and care, he succeeds in putting himself aside and focusing entirely on his help for Hannah. He raises himself above his physical condition and dedicates himself to her.

I learned that when he does so wholeheartedly and with a real desire, he manages to experience moments of loftiness. This is undeniably difficult.

As parents, it is easier for us to put step aside and concentrate on our children's needs, which is not the case with our partners. The book proved to me that it is possible even if it is challenging, and that it may be easier to do so if we accept our ability limits without comparing ourselves to others.

6. Giving to someone else is really giving to ourselves.

Shamosh decided to dedicate his life to Hannah. This decision raises the question what does he gain from it. Can we give our all to others without thinking about ourselves at all? Perhaps we actually do gain something.

I discovered that Shamosh did get something important in return. Hannah's love, which makes him so happy. This happiness gives him the strength to do what is most important to him, write. By dedicating his life to Hannah, he has gifted his life back again. Through their mutual love that means so much to him, and through his increased inner strength. Through love and strength, he can dedicate himself to work and use his daily life as inspiration for his writing.

I try to understand what I gift myself through caring for Adam, when I dedicate a considerable amount of my time and thoughts to him, and do things for him that he cannot do right now. I think that it makes me a better person and this, I believe, is significant.

When I think about all that I gained from this book, I cannot help but wonder whether I can put these beautiful insights into practice in my daily life. The love between Adam and me is not the same as that between Amnon and Hannah, and I am also not as patient and generous as Amnon.

I gain a lot of encouragement from my surroundings about the way I support Adam. However, when I read how Amnon supports Hannah, I feel that I am not good enough or compassionate enough. The feeling that I am not worthy comes up again, along with criticism and self-judgment.

If I find it hard to put these insights into practice, will my readers believe it is possible? I know that it is possible, and the comparisons that I draw between Shamosh and myself does not help. My premise is that most of us are good people who want to do our best. Each of us has his sensitive points, and when experiencing a setback, one reacts automatically in the way that one is used to whether that be with anger, impatience, fear, guilt or accusation.

When we do not manage to make a difference or achieve a goal that we set for ourselves, most of us judge ourselves in a way that we would never consider doing if a dear friend had experienced the same difficulty. When we judge ourselves, the situation is harder. We need time to exit the destructive cycle and to feel ready to start building anew.

Despite the doubts and because of my strong will, I choose to take advantage of the opportunities for growth and development that present themselves. I adopt Amnon and Hannah's model as I am able to , without judging my gains and failures.

DAILY LIFE – A TRAVELOGUE

How I cope with depression daily, in the style of a travelogue.

People have asked, and I have asked myself, why I chose to expose what we are going through and share our lives when the stories are often not particularly flattering. Writing my personal experiences in the form of a diary allows me to vent about my feelings. The act of writing down what I go through helps and makes it easier for me. The page is forgiving, allowing to put down the things that are hard to voice out loud.

Despite the difficulty that comes with exposure, I wish to provide people with meaningful insights that can help them. I believe that there are more advantages than potential setbacks in exposure. Just as I like reading true life stories, even if they are hard, I believe that many others do too.

Most importantly, I gain a huge amount from other people's stories. Through their stories, I discover new ways of coping. I am particularly encouraged by reading about peoples' setbacks, and the ways they cope and picked themselves up again. I feel the need share my knowledge on coping with the illness, my difficulties, failures, and overcoming hardships.

At a certain point, I felt uncomfortable with exposing Adam and other family members. I had Adam go over the manuscript before sending it to the editor and tell me how he felt about the exposure. He thought about it for a while and ultimately told me that he felt comfortable with it.

There is no reason to be ashamed of our past experiences, and I myself am full of pride about mine (not always happy, but definitely proud). I am a big believer in not being ashamed of anything, and most definitely at peace with my decision.

GOOD DAYS, LESS GOOD DAYS, AND BAD DAYS

Here are a few examples of different days from my diary, wishing to portray an authentic picture of the situation.

THURSDAY
Today I left Adam home alone for a whole day. In the morning before I left, we spoke in a new way, thanks to Shamosh's book. I felt that the insights that slowly seeped in as I read the book encouraged me to talk with Adam differently. For example- before reading the book, I would say, "You need to go for walks, if you do not, do not complain afterward." Today I said, "Adam, go for a walk- the weather is nice, and you can." See the difference?

I hugged and kissed him and left. I asked him if he loves me, and he answered that he does, but he does not love himself. I told him that he is a special person, and it is a shame that he does not realize that.

I went to see my ninety-seven-year-old father and afterward visited my son and grandchildren. Adam was alone from ten o' clock in the morning until eight-thirty at night. He was not in a good mood. He was scared and therefore was not capable of doing anything. Sometimes he says that he is not capable but does things anyway, and sometimes he says it and does not do anything. I came home tired and helped him prepare food for our Friday night family dinner with the children and grandchildren.

I know that the thought of their visit stresses him out. He behaves differently than the way he used to when he was an active partner and happy to meet the children and grandchildren. By the time we had finished preparing the food, he had somewhat calmed down.

FRIDAY (A WEEK LATER)
Things are not good. Adam has been in a depressive episode for half a year. Today is Friday, and we are after ten Transcranial Magnetic Stimulation (TMS) treatments (for an explanation, refer to the chapter on "Different Treatments that Adam Received during Depression").

We take a short trip to the Hospital every day for the treatment.

We decided to try this treatment because we feel hopeless. The pills are not helping, neither did hospitalization (Adam was hospitalized for about three weeks). We are unsatisfied with our psychiatrist because he does not initiate anything- instead, he asks us for new ideas of how to speed up treatment. He recommended the TMS treatment, so we decided to try it. Our oldest daughter read about it. It claimed a seventy percent success rate.

We decided to try it despite the expense and despite the trips to Tel Aviv which were uncomfortable in the August heat. We were told that we could notice an improvement from the seventh treatment, and to pay attention to any small change. Three days ago, we noticed a slight improvement. Adam was aware of his surroundings and enjoyed being with our grandchildren who came to visit. But yesterday evening, he once again felt really awful, and this morning he woke up in a terrible mood and annoyed me with his demands .

On good days, our relationship is of the "live and let live" variety, but when Adam is in a depressive episode, he suddenly cannot stand all kinds of things that do not bother me. For example, if there is no food made or there are a few dishes in the sink, he finds it unbearable.

I am distressed by the heat and the daily trips. The sleeping pill I took three days ago still left me groggy yesterday. I have no patience nor strength for his sudden demands. In short, things are not good, and I beginning to doubt the point of continuing with the book which looks to prove that it is possible to live well despite the situation. I feel suffocated and want to run away. Adam wants to die; he has no more strength, and he is still worried about there being no food made for today and tomorrow, and is blaming me. I do not want to deal with food right now, just to feel free.

I cannot leave him, even for a few hours, so how can I write a book which gives advice to others?

We are in a downward spiral.

After traveling day after day for two weeks, in the heat, by train and taxis to Tel Aviv, I was looking to rest on Friday and Saturday. But when I am anxious and worried, I cannot relax.

I tried a new recipe that I found on the internet to calm Adam, and to have some food in the house. Trying to calm myself after crying which made me feel weak and tired, I got into bed to read a little and nap. Being away and alone is good for me. It is just a shame that I had not realized that before getting annoyed.

The ability to distance oneself before getting annoyed is vital. We deserve it, and it is so important, even if our partners try to stop us in different ways, by trying to arouse pity, or asking for things that we cannot deliver.

Today I sent a question to the director of the psychiatry department. I asked him whether a seventy-five-year-old person who has had a stroke in the past could go through electroconvulsive therapy. He answered that there is no reason why not. It is encouraging to know that there are other options to try, even if it scares us somehow.

In the meantime, we decided to wait for the results after the psychiatrist increased Adam's dosage of Lamotrigine. If it did not help, we will explore the option of electroconvulsive therapy.

I am worried that Adam does not have the strength to keep suffering. We changed psychiatrists, for a young one who impressed us both. On our first visit, she said something which really encouraged us, "Don't worry, you will get over this."

SUNDAY
Today I arranged a meeting with Deborah, the book editor. I shared that things are not good right now and that if I visit her, I may burst out crying. I was happy when she said that I am welcome, and that I should not be alone when I am having such a hard time. . I was so happy with her answer yet burst out crying again because I feel so alone. I do not want to tell my children what is going on, especially not my son who is moving house.

After two days feeling so down, I decided to turn to my Focusing teacher, Orna. She always helps me understand what has suddenly gone wrong, what knocked me down and pushed me back to darker days. Indeed, after just a few minutes into the meeting, I understood that it is okay to be sad. Behind the difficulty I have been experiencing lies my disappointment in myself, for being sad and not being able to stay happy for my family in these challenging times.

Besides being sad, I also felt disappointed in myself for not keeping my promise to be strong and happy. I had decided that it was enough that Adam feels sad, so my role should be to be happy and strong. But it proved to be too much for me. All of that was, of course, in addition to other difficult conclusions such as, "Once again, I am inadequate. I decided to write a book, told people about it, and what will happen now? Another disappointment." I regressed to the days of needing to do things instead of going with the flow and accepting whatever comes along. I went back to thinking about whether what I was doing was okay, and wondering what others think about me. I went back to the old patterns.

As a result of all of this, I decided to change the title of my book to Better Days, Worse Days: Supporting a Depressed Partner Without Losing Your Light. Sometimes it is about thriving, and at other times, it is just about living.

The speed at which I returned to clear my cloudy thinking was incredible. In the meeting, I talked about my feelings of loneliness. At the end she said: "Doki, this meeting is my gift to you. You do not need to pay, and you can call me whenever you need to." It chased away my loneliness.

FRIDAY

Today everyone is coming for the weekend, so we need to prepare. Adam made some amazing stuffed vegetables and delicious round pastries. It has been so long since he prepared food, and it came out so well. I complimented him, and he was pleased.

I try to absorb strength from the sea, which has a wonderful effect on me. Soon everyone will arrive, and their presence- especially the little ones, gives me a lot of strength. I notice that Adam pays more attention to the little ones than before, which is obviously encouraging. Occasionally, he says that he is anxious and takes medication, but I notice what is happening and I think I can see a difference.

I still feel the serenity, the love for Adam, the acceptance of reality. We hug more, and this obviously gives me strength.

SATURDAY

Saturday arrives, and so does the anger. Adam is withdrawn and does not notice any of my hard work. Once again, I fall into anger, disappointment, and victimhood. This is it? The new beginning is over? It has only just began. Perhaps I should have been angry with Adam. I do not think that anger is always a bad thing. Sometimes, it is the right thing, and making an effort not to get angry can feel worse.

However, getting angry in the right way and place is to be angry about something specific and then move on. I could not move on because I felt anger as well as hopelessness, returning so quickly to the familiar, old hard place.

It was a wonderful Saturday. We went to the beach; we ate; the children played, and we enjoyed spending time together. It really was a delight, apart from my anger at Adam.

SUNDAY

It's already Sunday. I am still a little angry with Adam, but we talked things through, and soon the good feelings return. It makes me so happy. Still, I know and understand that there will be more pitfalls along the way.

Suddenly, the book deals more with our relationship than with depression. I did not intend to write a book about relationships but I believe that a loving relationship can change the way a person, suffering from depression, feels and have a positive impact on him, so I choose to devote time to the subject.

Adam still says that he is having a hard time and he is anxious, he takes tranquilizers. Despite this, I view his activities as a reliable gauge of his state.

He woke up this morning to discover that the infection he has suffered from for years, flared up again (an infection that penetrated a bone following operations on a broken leg). When it flares up, Adam needs to see a doctor immediately, have blood tests, get his leg bandaged, and x-rayed. He went for these procedures all by himself, though each was in a different place. This was a good sign.

TUESDAY

Orna comes every day to work with Adam, and today she came too. She sits with him for an hour and a half. I am so happy about this set-up, as I trust her entirely. From meeting to meeting, they get to know each other better, become closer, and hone in on their focus. At the end of the meeting, they let me know what happened and what decisions they reached. Adam calls her "the angel."

Tomorrow I will leave Adam alone for four nights, to go with my daughter to Corfu. Our two other children will take turns to be with Adam, and occasionally he will be alone. It may do him good, or not.

Today I got in touch with Amnon Shamosh. I told him how his book affected me, and we decided to meet up soon. My oldest daughter lives on a Kibbutz up in the north,- not far from where Amnon lives. We visit her once every three weeks for two to three days each time. I want to give Amnon a copy of my first book, and ask him what else he can teach me about relationships in times of illness.

THURSDAY
The last two days have been very hard for Adam. Tonight I am leaving for four nights, it is hard for me to leave him in his current state. Today we had good friends, from Tel Aviv, who came to visit, and we had an enjoyable time, but Adam once again retreated into a dark place.

Yesterday I realized that it has been eight months since the depression started. A long time. Adam is withdrawn and not capable of being with anyone else, and it is so apparent because taking notice of others and complimenting them was always so characteristic of him in the past.

I enjoy myself in Corfu with my daughter, and our other two children take turns to be with Adam. They give us strength, togetherness, caring, and love, which means so much. I know that it is hard for Adam, but I tell myself that this is my opportunity to enjoy every moment, which we most definitely do. I hope for a change for the better for Adam.

On Monday, the day after I get back, we will meet a neuroscientist. He gave a talk two weeks ago to a group that we are part of. Her talk was fascinating, she spoke about a method that she developed and now uses with her patients. Once I realized that she accepts patients, I approached her and asked if she could work with Adam, and we arranged a meeting. On Monday, we will also meet our geriatrician, whom we both like a lot. On Wednesday, we will meet the psychiatrist, to decide what our next steps will be. When I get home, I intend to speak with a woman who was in the hospital at the same time as Adam and received electroconvulsive therapy.

All of these provide a ray of hope that we have new treatment possibilities for Adam.

MONDAY

Finally, the day I have been waiting for arrives; the visit to the neuroscientist who will start working with Adam. Adam was in a terrible mood and hardly cooperated. I got annoyed with him, and felt that I had no more energy to cope with him. He was apathetic, hardly answered, and when we got there, after a half-hour journey, he was in a very anxious state. Ten minutes later, we left, he said he could not stay any longer.

I hated him and could have strangled him. Once again, my well-intended plans fail. Like a cow that fills up the milk jug and, in the end, kicks the jug over. I am very agitated, but suddenly I stop wrestling with myself and allow myself to be angry and to hate, and I calm down.

Luckily, later that day we met with our incredible geriatrician, who noticed that I was agitated and had been crying. She spoke to Adam, saying that there was no need to be afraid of the anxiety attacks because they are not dangerous. She then turned to me and said, "You have worn yourself out, and if we will not take care of you, everything is going to tumble down. You need to stop carrying everything on your shoulders, and stop looking for solutions. Adam will take care of himself, and nothing will happen. From now on, stop worrying about plans, you can go free. You are allowed to hate him and be angry with him sometimes. You're allowed." It was such a good feeling to be noticed by someone and realize that nothing will happen if I choose to let go.

What she said reinforced what Deborah, the editor, said a few days earlier in our meeting. She said, "Doki, you can't go on like this. You are constantly busy providing support. You support the whole project surrounding Adam, the family, and yourself. You cannot go on like this. You have to let go, allow yourself to fall apart, cry, be sad, be afraid, and be weak. It may be scary, but you are constantly trying too hard. Every time there is a downfall, you are quick to get up and continue supporting."

Two people, both close to me and whom I respect, said the same thing. They said that I must rest, let go, not hold on, allow myself to fall apart, not take responsibility for everything, not look for solutions, and allow myself to feel weak. I am allowed to not know, cry, fear, be angry, and anything else that may come up. I promised Deborah, the doctor, and myself that I will act on their words.

WEDNESDAY

I visited my father today, and on the way, the sadness welled up inside. I did not try to push it away. I gave it space, and nothing happened to me. I was not happy and strong; I did not feel that I needed to pretend that I felt okay.

I went back home and did not rush to see what was happening with Adam or start looking for solutions to solve problems. I did not hide from him that I was weak and sad. I think that it could be helpful for both of us if I accept these feelings instead of being hard on myself because of them. I am learning how to feel weak and sad and to be okay with that, not to hide it and carry on with my head held high. I think that this gives me strength and improves my health. I am breathing steadily. Suddenly, I am not worried about failing or any other catastrophes. I am learning to fail and to be okay with it. When I truly allow myself to be there, something happens, something fascinating and sweet.

Thank you, Adam- for helping me learn and experience something that once scared me so much. Suddenly, something that I once found so threatening turned into something else. I always taught others to accept whatever presents itself without fighting it. All of the methods that I have learned in recent years, Focusing, Gestalt, The Work method, and Tapping (EFT),- teach this same approach. However, this time, I took things up another level in my willingness to be in that place. Perhaps I can do so even more. I hope so, because, suddenly, it is very appealing.

In the evening, we met up with our group. In the past, if I were not in a good mood, I avoided going because with others, I was used to being happy, laughing, contributing, and I would be embarrassed to be in a bad mood. This time I came feeling sad and, this may sound strange, but I was happy about feeling sad, I enjoyed myself. It is not as if I have finished working on myself; I do not believe there is such a thing. Nevertheless, every small step leads to a feeling of immense wellness.

SUNDAY

We are experiencing difficult days. We cannot see any improvement in Adam's situation and are considering electroconvulsive therapy. I am not in a good mood. I have had enough. Adam fell from a chair last night and hit his head. I was asleep and did not hear a thing, and he lay on the floor for half an hour until he summoned the strength to get up.

WEDNESDAY

A few more days have gone by, and perhaps there is a slight change in Adam's mood. We are all happy that there may be change, but I notice that we are careful not to celebrate prematurely. We have been disappointed quite a few times, and have forgotten that things could be good, like in the past.

If there is a change, is it because of the increased medication and lithium this past week? Perhaps Adam felt that I am close to breaking point. Maybe the blow to the head did something. We will wait to see what the coming days bring, and then we will have a better idea. I remind myself that even if things improve, they will not return to how they were before.

Adam is suffering physically, too. He is unsteady, weak, and in the beginning stages of Parkinson's. All of this affects his mood because he does not link all that to the changes he is going through. I need to be honest with myself. Things will not return to how they were before. I too will not go back to how I was before. I am weaker, more tired, and we are simply getting older. It is difficult to accept this, and it is very frightening. Just as it scares Adam, it scares me too. We need to start appreciating even a slight improvement.

I took a few days off from writing the book. Suddenly, I do not want to write. It may be because I was waiting for a real improvement before continuing, only to discover that Adam is not on the road to overcome his depression. After a day and a half of seeming improvement, we experienced another slump. His legs are not stable and cannot support him, which pushes him back to depression.

I have given up hope. This is a powerful statement. Yes, it is hard to build up hope only to be disappointed, repeatedly.

I find I am also less energetic. I stay in bed a lot, not doing much. Perhaps my age is finally catching up with me, or maybe I feel that something is ending and might not return. That "thing" is our relationship, not the relationship itself, but activities that we do together as a couple. It is hard to get Adam to go out to do spontaneous activities. Sometimes he will come with me to the cinema, but not much more than that. It is hard for me. It is the festivals season but we are staying home, with not that many close friends here where we live.

Friends of ours from Jerusalem moved to Tel Aviv, which is closer. We meet up with them occasionally for dinner, at either our place or theirs. These meetings are enjoyable and fill us with happiness and love. Adam also enjoys meeting old friends. At our last meeting, he was already experiencing depression and was very quiet, unlike in the past when he would tell jokes and make us laugh.

Now it is our turn to host, and, understandably, we push it off because of Adam's condition. Eventually, I decide not to push it off anymore. I need friendship. Adam needs it too, even if it is hard for him. I call and set it up.

***

Adam tells me that he thinks a lot about death and it worries him. In the last few years, Adam lost three close sisters. Growing up he had ten siblings. People who suffer from depression tend to think about death and sometimes wish to die. Each time we visited a doctor and spoke about his depression, the question of whether Adam had plans to kill himself would immediately come up. Yet, he has never planned on killing himself. I asked him a question that he found hard to answer, "Could it be that you want to reunite with your sisters?" He said no, it is hard for him to live with depression, day in and day out. He is in constant conflict, on the one hand, he has had enough of this way of life, and on the other, he knows that a different kind of life does exist which he can enjoy.

He said that he is not capable of killing himself, because of what this would do to his loved ones. I asked him if this means that he is suffering on our behalf, and pointed out how paradoxical that is, as we also suffer when he suffers.

Death is the ultimate emptying out of everything we are, our physical and spiritual definitions. Depression is also an emptying out of everything we are. Which is harder to cope with, the fear of death or life under depression? Someone who suffers from depression feels dead while alive. Life is scary and turns to permanent fear.

MONDAY
Adam's mood has been better over the last few days. I think he is no longer in a deep depression like before. He is a bit down about his physical condition, but this is far from his previous depression. I notice that from the way he acts around our grandchildren, he is having fun with them in a way that he was not capable of before and is talking in a louder voice. He is far from the happy person he used to be, but there is, undeniably, an improvement.

Last weekend he came with me to the Kibbutz to see our oldest daughter, it has been a long time since that happened. He even prepared a wonderful meal for them. I like going there. We stay in a guest room under our daughter's house, so we have our own space. I went by myself many times when

Adam did not want to join me. Nowadays, I don't leave him alone. I have not been to our daughter for a few months, and it was so wonderful to see her again. His legs problems gets him down, he cannot stand. But still this is nothing like his earlier depression.

He is still considering electroconvulsive therapy. I think that if there is an improvement, then it's better to hold off for now. It is an intensive treatment, and I am a little afraid. This Friday, we have a meeting with the psychiatrist, and will decide together.

We also went to see the geriatrician. Adam also went to see the occupational therapist, who checked him, asked questions, and suggested activities he should focus on such as activities together with other people. There are senior social clubs where we live, that offer varied activities for people his age. It would be wonderful if he were to agree to go.

Adam sometimes complains about feeling a lack of purpose, so this could be a great solution. I do not mind accompanying him sometimes, but I do not want to pressure him about it. He has started seeing his physiotherapist again, and wants to try to join a Pilates class. If all of this goes to plan, we will be progressing.

THURSDAY
I have started planning my eight-day trip to Tanzania with my oldest grandson. Only another four days until we are off, it is

getting closer. I am so excited to spend time with him. I am very close to him despite him being a teenager. Even if just grunts when I ask him something, it does not bother me, I am happy even when we are quiet.

Apart from a driver, we are traveling alone. My grandson insisted on not joining a group.

I hope that Adam will be okay on his own for some of the time. He refused to have anyone stay with him. The children will visit him, but they will not be around every day. Our son-in-law, my grandson's father, whom I am travelling with will spend the most time with him. Adam has dreamed for years of taking our oldest grandchild on a safari for his Bar Mitzvah. It must be hard for him that, in the end, he cannot travel and that I am taking him instead.

The week we spent in Tanzania and Zanzibar was incredible. The safari was an opportunity to experience nature in all its glory and was incredibly uplifting. We spent three days in Zanzibar resting and enjoying ourselves together. My grandson and I got on so well; I managed to disconnect from everything I am going through and enjoyed myself without a second thought. I adore trips, love adventures, and am happy to meet new people.

I felt that I had aged; my energy levels were not what they used to be. I don't believe I will be able to go on a similar trip with my granddaughter wandering around for hours on end. Still, going on trips and vacations is the ultimate pleasure for me, and I do have people with whom to do it, friends, my sisters, my children, my grandchildren, and even by myself.

I hope that Adam will be able to join me, but if his condition does not improve, I am not sure he will be able to.

What caught my eye in Zanzibar, which, I believe are linked to depression, were the intense poverty, the wretchedness, and the incredibly difficult living conditions of the locals. It was hard to witness. Nevertheless, the local people were happy and welcoming. Maybe because of their togetherness. They were always in small groups, standing together, sitting together, and walking together. They spend most of the time, outside so I believe that this community tightness protects them from loneliness and depression.

Adam spent the week with our dear son-in-law, and things were good for him. He made sure to go for walks around the neighborhood with him, and said that he did not feel bad at all.

Returning home was hard. On the trip, I felt free. It was just the two of us, and I was responsible for initiating things. I found it easy, and it all went smoothly. When I returned home, the gap between my vivaciousness and Adam's slowness was even more prominent.

While I was away, Adam had to take care of some important, medical-related issues, but did nothing about it. I got annoyed and scared as I understood that the situation was going to get worse rather than improve. Though the depression has actually improved Adam's physical condition, his lack of orderliness, forgetfulness, and slowness got worse.

It took me a while to mull over and accept the reality of the situation, having to go on doing what we can and have to do. My eldest daughter was staying with us, and was very angry with me for not being nice to him. Yes, I was frightened, and when I am frightened, that is how I behave.

FRIDAY

The distance between us is not getting any closer, on the contrary it keeps widening. I have to accept this, just as Adam should accept his condition. I feel that this is the biggest issue, the fact that he is not ready to come to terms with his physical condition. Orna explained that he is going through a process of mourning for his body,-which will not return to what it once was.

Today, I returned after visiting my father and, later on, my son. I helped my son put his daughters to bed, and had a good time. It warmed my heart when my three-year-old granddaughter ran to me and cried, "Grandma, I missed you. I love you." It gives me so much strength.

MONDAY

Today was difficult. I feel as if my life is in ruins, and I am angry., I tried to reason with myself trying to stop feeling so down. Thoughts like "it happens"; "it could have happened to you too," "you are not immune from this happening to you too," "how would you feel if, in addition to what you were going through, people were angry and impatient with you?"

Later, I told myself that I should not be looking for solutions or excuses as I am allowed to feel down. So this is how I feel today, going through a kind of mourning process, feeling that my life is in ruins. I cry about my fate, unable to be comforted. My life is not as I imagined it would be.

There are also moments when I feel happy, proud, satisfied and pleased. Nevertheless, my life with Adam will not be what I thought it would be. Our life together will focus on his health, visiting doctors, making sure he keeps active and constantly worry about his condition. Not taking trips together, nor enjoying his lovely cooking, or treating me the way he used to, and all the things he used to happily do for our home and the children.

I am seventy-one years old, and most certainly feel my age. Traveling on bush trails on the safari was hard for me. It is not really suitable for someone my stage, but I feel young in spirit and sometimes feel like a child, not wishing to stop my plans.

I am busy with various activities and do much of what I want to do, but I find myself increasingly involved in Adam's health. We have gone through similar times in the past, when Adam had cancer, or went through a back operation following a time of incredible pain, when he fell from a ladder and spent seven months in the hospital, and was operated on five times. These were challenging times. Those times passed with times of quiet followed. Now I understand that there will not be another quiet period. This is it; we are living alongside illness.

I do not know what awaits us. His physical deterioration may stop or may, G-d forbid, get worse. I do not know how either of these scenarios will play out and affect us.

I know that even though I despair occasionally, I will get up because that is how I am. I have acquired many tools throughout my life that help me overcome anger, despair, impatience, and loneliness to recapture my enjoyment of life and love. Today, though, I am ending the day feeling heaviness and uncertainty about our future. Whatever will be, this is my life, and I will live it fully.

Some Final Thoughts

Life is a journey. We do not always reach the final destination that we imagined we would. Perhaps the main conclusion we can arrive at is that we should not be planning our final goal as each day is a vital step on our path of life and a goal in and of itself.

Of course, we want the depression to pass, and in most cases, it eventually does. However, it does not guarantee it will not return. Life is complicated, yet it also presents us, perhaps specifically through the challenging situations we face, with many opportunities to grow, reveal, experience excitement, and other meaningful things that broaden our hearts. I like to compare the process to a journey because a journey involves moments of curiosity, discovery, and enjoyment, as well as moments of getting lost, fatigue, fear of strange places and more. The same is true for an inner journey. I refuse to give up on either of these journeys. If I had to choose between them, I would choose the inner journey, which is an inseparable part of coping with a challenging situation.

I feel the need to finish this book on an optimistic note because we are feeling more optimistic in recent days. Adam is starting to accept his physical condition. Recently he said, "If I have to choose between depression and serious leg problems, I prefer the serious leg problems." His mood is improving and so is mine.

I am writing this additional chapter about two weeks after I have finished writing the book: Adam has not been in depression for about three weeks, and it has been wonderful. But, we had not tasted the sweetness of rest between dealing with depression and Parkinson's, as there was overlap between them.

As of late, I realized that when things are hard for me, I allow myself to mourn. I have learned how to mourn. Mourning does not mean constantly thinking about how difficult or frightening something is. It also does not mean running away from something or persuading myself that things could be much worse and that I should enjoy every moment, and so on. It means letting the feeling be.

I have noticed that this allows me to bear these feelings and be in charge of them instead of allowing them to be in charge of me. I allow the feeling of mourning to exist for as long as it needs to, usually several hours, and then I calm down and go back to being happy and strong.

My support for my dear husband is crucial. We continue to live and do whatever is possible together, and what is not possible to do together, we do alone. I got ballroom dancing videos that help improve movement for people with Parkinson's. They also boost our morale and we plan to dance for half an hour every day.

I turned to the National Insurance Institute and requested a caregiver, despite us not being ready for one. I want to prepare for any possible deterioration. I found a service that provides help by the hour which I could use if I need to leave Adam alone.

I am so happy that I dedicated a large part of my life to self-growth and that I coped in the best way possible with barriers that stood in my way. I am sure that this helps me cope today as I support my dear ones, especially myself.

Finally, I would like to refer to a poem by Aaron Bass on emotional first aid. Bass' poem cleverly paints a scene where physical aspects of first aid care: paramedics, bandages, and vaccinations, are replaced by expressions of love, compassion, hugs, and kisses. Bass describes a Healer of hearts who looks into the hearts of those hurt, massages their hearts, and brings them back to life with love.

I think that it would be easier to face life's difficulties, especially in the case of depression, if we could adopt the ideas that Bass expresses in this wonderful poem. Too often, when things are hard and painful, and when one is depressed, we feel ashamed which makes the situation far worse. If only we could muster up compassion, love and hugs, we would be in a far better place.

APPENDIX 1: TREATMENTS THAT ADAM RECEIVED DURING HIS DEPRESSION

Which medical and alternative treatments did we try? Perhaps it would be easier to ask which treatments we did not try!

In the past six months we have been through a lot. We tried many different things and experienced many disappointments along the way.

Adam went to a psychiatrist, who prescribed medication. We simultaneously tried the Alpha-Stim, a medical device that treats pain, stress, and depression through electrotherapy, used for twenty minutes a day. We rented one for several months, and Adam used it daily.

We rented it from a person who told us that he had suffered from depression for years. He reached the conclusion that the medication used to treat depression worsens it. He decided to stop taking his medication and to do inner work instead. He has not taken medication for several years and has not suffered from depression during that time.

After we spoke, I returned home with many questions, wondering whether Adam should stop taking his medication. I thought that the man's claim,-that the medicine, with all its side effects, could be the source of many problems, made sense, but I was not sure if Adam should stop taking them.

It was not the first time I heard about people who stopped taking medication, did inner work, and no longer suffered from depression. I knew that in the same way that I had done inner work to cope with the feeling of worthlessness, it was possible to work on the things that lead to depression (false beliefs, mistaken perceptions, and so on), but was not sure whether it would be right for Adam.

The fact that others took the self-work route and succeeded, does not mean that every person can do it. Therefore, we decided not to stop the medication at this point.

Adam's psychiatrist reached the point where he did not know how else he could help, so he referred us to the psychiatric unit in the hospital for further consultation. After we met with the head of the department, we decided that if things did not improve in the next couple of weeks, Adam would check in. His condition was unbearable, so we ended up deciding that there was no point in waiting a couple of weeks, Adam checked into the hospital.

He stayed in an open ward, which was hard for him. Two things were especially so. Firstly, Adam is fastidious about cleanliness, and the condition of the rooms, specifically the bathroom, was far from satisfactory for him. He had spent time in hospitals before, after operations, with far better conditions than those in this one. Secondly, Adam finds it hard to stand and walk, and there were no special facilities in the shower to help, not even hooks for towels and clothes. We found it strange that such a large, sophisticated hospital has such inferior conditions, especially since it would be easy to fix the issues.

Another thing that Adam found hard was the social aspect. Adam, by nature, is a very social person, but not when he suffers from depression. The ward had about thirty patients of varying ages, many of whom were young and got on well together.

One of the things that helps during hospitalization in this kind of ward is being with good people, who suffer from the same, or similar, problem. Just like in any society, social groups form on hospital wards too. It was hard for Adam to initialize conversation, so I asked the attending psychiatrist to introduce him to someone who had more experience and could help him. She thought it was a good idea, but nothing came of it for some reason.

Patients are not usually allowed to go home on the first weekend of their hospitalization or to leave the ward and walk around in the first few days. In Adam's case, they allowed him to go home for the first weekend, on condition that he return to the ward. They were worried that he would not want to return.

Despite the hardships, Adam understood that he needed to give things a chance, and he checked into the hospital again. Slowly but surely, and with our help, he started getting to know people, getting closer to some of them, and feeling a little better.

We spent every day there with him: the children, our friends, my sisters, and me. He was somewhat embarrassed about being there but managed to stand it for about three weeks. We noticed a tangible improvement in his mood during his time there, but it worsened the closer he got to his discharging date. His physical condition deteriorated, and he had trouble walking. His hands shook, and he was diagnosed with Parkinson's. It was quite a blow because we were already dealing with so much. The hospital increased his medication, and we went home.

At home, his condition got worse. Adam claimed that his physical deterioration caused his bad mood. He fell a few times from the bed, and we started thinking that we may have to hire a caregiver to look after him. We did not know what to do and felt discouraged.

I decided to ask our friend, a pharmacist who wrote a book about medication and the danger of combining certain medications, for help. She visited us, looked over Adam's list of medicines and dosages, and suggested that we contact an international specialist to advise us how to reduce the amount of medication. She thought that some of the medication that the doctors added in the hospital cause symptoms of Parkinson's, and since Adam's mood has not improved, it could be worth thinking about stopping some of them under the guidance of a professional. She explained though that it could, for a while worsen his depression.

She asked Adam if he would be willing to give it a try, and Adam, after consideration, decided that yes, he would. We met with the specialist who referred us to a local doctor who works according to his method. It turned out that this was our geriatrician, considering how happy we are with her, we were happy to consult her.

With her help, Adam gradually stopped taking some medication, and after some time, the symptoms related to Parkinson's disappeared completely. We were happy because these symptoms greatly bothered and scared Adam.

Adam's depression got worse. We kept looking for other ways of treating it. We tried the "Hadassah" pill, also known as "The Alternative Happiness Pill", which studies have proved helps greatly during depression.

We worked with both a physiotherapist and a fitness instructor twice a week, and Adam received regular hydrotherapy treatments. Nothing helped Adam break free from his depression.

We then turned to Transcranial Magnetic Stimulation (TMS) treatment; a daily treatment administered in the hospital that lasts for a month. The patient wears a kind of helmet and magnetic pulses are sent to the part of the brain responsible for the depression. We tried this treatment as we heard that there is a seventy percent success rate, and after consultation, we decided to try it. It was a hard month. It was August, the hottest month of the year and traveling to the hospital every day on trains and in taxis was a real hardship. The staff was excellent, and said we might notice an improvement as soon as the seventh treatment.

Before starting the treatment, we changed psychiatrists. Adam has seen our psychiatrist for a year and a half, and he was okay, but we felt that we needed someone who could suggest new treatment options and give us a stronger feeling of support. We started seeing a young psychiatrist and immediately left hopeful. She was a doctor in our local clinic, which meant that we saved a lot of money,- an important factor at the time. She encouraged Adam, saying, "This too will pass."

She thought that increasing Adam's dosage of medication could be the right step, but around that time, we had just decided to try TMS treatment, so she pushed off increasing the dosage, opting to wait and see how the treatment goes.

Near the end of the TMS treatment with no improvement, we decided to start the increased dosage of his medication, despite being aware that the effect of the TMS treatment may not be apparent until later on.

As of now, we are waiting and hoping to see an improvement.

***

Things did improve. From our many years of experience, we know that the medication helps. It is just hard, when experiencing depression, to sit and wait for it to take effect without doing anything else. There is always the fear of the medication not helping and finding ourselves needing to try something else. With Adam's , the medication always starts working long after the time noted on the prescription. Then suddenly, one day, we notice that the past few days have been good days. Then we celebrate, it is behind us, at least for now.

Even if the depression will return at some point, the reprieve is very comforting and allows for a period of relaxation and regaining strength.

APPENDIX 2: RECOMMENDED TOOLS FOR SELF-AWARENESS[7]

I wish to recommend a few tools that I use both in life and in my work when I help others in their self-awareness and change journey.

I recommend these tools because they are experiential, simple to understand and implement, and at the same time profound. Most importantly, they help build self-worth and self-acceptance. There are, of course, many more methods, but it is beyond the scope of this book to bring them all.

Focusing

The Focusing method[8] offers the possibility of taking a deep look inside ourselves, listening intently to the feelings that rise inside our body and to the inner truth hidden within.

---

7   This chapter appeared in my first book "An Equally Worthy Child" (Focus Publishing: 2018)

8   Ann Weiser Cornell, *The Power of Focusing* (New Harbinger Publications, 1996) Eugene Gendlin, *Focusing* (Bantam Doubleday Dell Publishing Group Inc., 1982)

The process is simple. It is deep and leads to a sense of release and the opportunity to make changes. In recent years, many professionals have adopted the method, and it became part of the mental therapeutic techniques used worldwide. It is an experiential and innovative method in that it claims the body, and not just the brain, thinks, and tells us a lot.

The quiet listening process (the Focusing trainer listens to the one Focusing, and the one Focusing listens to himself) is non-judgmental and allows space where it is possible to "just be," breathe and expand. It creates a space in which the hidden can reveal itself, express itself and where the person can renew his energies that flow from his touching his deep inner truth.

Focusing is a way of being. It is a technique for self-awareness, as well as a philosophy and a way of life. When Focusing one practices listening to or contemplating one's inner self. A dialogue and a relationship develops between him and those inner places that need to change or heal. The technique is effective, simple, and surprisingly powerful. It helps the focusing one to be aware at every moment of how he is feeling.

During the session the Focusing one talks about the difficulty he is experiencing. The Focusing trainer asks him to pay attention to the difficulty related feelings arising in his body. The Focusing one allows room for his feelings without judging. He understands that this is the right feeling at that moment, even if, in other situations, he is used to being embarrassed by it, ignoring or fighting it. He allows it to "be", trying to find the best word to describe it, and discover what he is scared of.

This process allows us to accept the feelings and parts of us we could not accept before, and to reach wholeness. The result is self-acceptance and self-value.

Byron Katie's Work Method

The basis of the Work Method lies in understanding that the suffering in our lives is caused entirely by us thinking and believing that reality needs to be different from what it is. According to this method, we suffer when we believe in thoughts that argue with reality. It teaches a simple and powerful investigation method whereby you can identify and study the thoughts that cause suffering in your world, learn what causes you pain and what you can do to set yourself free from the suffering.

The Work Method helps us accept ourselves as we are now, rather than how we believe we need to be. The questioning is experiential and includes four questions and three turnarounds. When doing the method, you write a sentence on a worksheet that you believe to be true and that causes you to suffer. . It can be about someone else (such as, "My husband does not respect me," or "My daughter needs to be more obedient") or about oneself (such as, "I am lazy," "I am stupid," "I am not sociable"). The process guide helps the person going through it, to identify the thought which is blocking him and causing his suffering with the following four questions and turnarounds.

The four questions are:

1. Is it true?
2. Are you absolutely sure that it is true?
3. How do you react when you believe in that thought?
4. Who would you be without that thought?

The turnarounds (one or three) refer to the sentence that one is questioning. For example, if the sentence we are checking is, "She needs to respect me," then there are three possible turnarounds:

1. I need to respect myself
2. She does not need to respect me
3. I need to respect her

You need to come up with examples for each turnaround or explain why it is correct. You should refer to each sentence when you are in a meditative state and carrying out an inner examination. In this way, what seems to be a difficulty often turns to an opportunity or an experience. New insights and ideas surface.

Many people who use the method feel that the results changed their lives.

The investigation can help us release beliefs that we have adopted which cause us suffering. It can also peel away masks that we have put on, that might have helped or even saved us at some point but are no longer relevant now. Through all of this, we connect to our inner truth and ourselves, accept ourselves as we are, and awaken a sense of self-worth.

The Gestalt Method

This method focuses on the person and the uniqueness of one's experience. The main concepts of the method include focusing on the present, speaking in first person, speaking in the present tense about every subject that comes up; holding a dialogue between different parts within us to bring them closer to one another to enable choices; and not remaining at extremities that do not allow for freedom of choice.

The basic assumption of Gestalt is that a person is a holistic organism with an unlimited potential for growth and development, who has the power to achieve self-actualization despite injury or disability.

While going through the process, we identify true needs and differentiate between them, and those that are not true. We learn to take responsibility for the parts of ourselves that we have disposed of, and to let go of parts that are not ours. In such a way, we connect to our True Self, which allows for feelings of freedom, powerfulness, self-acceptance and liberation from suffering.

APPENDIX 3: THE CONNECTION BETWEEN THE TWO BOOKS

After this book was published in Hebrew, and before it was translated into English, I gave a lecture on the connection between the two (An Equally Worthy Child and Living with a Depressed Spouse and Surviving

I suddenly realized how closely the two books are connected, and I wished to highlight this connection as an addition to this English translation.

The first book, "An Equally Worthy Child" talks about our feelings of self-worth and the fact that we are all born as diamonds.

Brandon Bays, the founder of The Journey Method, coined this description. Each one is born a diamond, and, slowly but surely, the diamond gets dirty and covered in mud. We are all born equally worthy, and are still different from one another. We are born precise but our environment affects us, trying to correct us out of fear of us not fitting into society, or out of fear of us not succeeding if we carry on being the way we are.

The people doing this (parents, teachers) generally have good intentions, but the result is that we grow up somewhat repressed. Our parents, or caregivers, try to get rid of characteristics or behaviors that they believe will harm us in life. They encourage characteristics or behaviors that they believe will serve us better later on in life, such as teaching us that it is not good to be angry or be embarrassed. They do this by using words such as, "need", and "should not", one "needs" to do such and such, and one "should not" do so and so. These remarks vary from one family to the other, according to what is acceptable and valued in that household and the society one is living in. In one household, you might hear, "You need to be angry, and should not keep quiet," whereas, in another, you may hear, "You need to keep quiet, and not get angry."

As children, we are dependent on our caregivers and absorb everything they tell us. We end up absorbing and absorbing on the one hand, and throwing up and throwing up on the other.

Then we grow up and are not satisfied with ourselves because a part of us is not actually us. The strange thing is that the only way to feel good is to be just as we are, and accept ourselves as such. We need to develop, change, and understand that we are fine just as we are, and not change because we are not good enough.

When we feel that we are worthy just as we are, then we can dare. Then we can express every part of ourselves, our feelings, thoughts, desires, and needs. We can get close to people without worrying about rejection. We can experience genuine conversations with others. There is nothing stopping us. We can live life fully.

I am reminded of a Hebrew song, loosely translated as, "Just As I Am" - written by Shai Or, and sung by his daughter. It is a lovely song and I would recommend playing it for your children and grandchildren.

I realized that what I wrote about in my first book could help build emotional resilience. That, in turn, builds physical resilience. It may even help prevent illness, and this prevention could be the most valuable aspect of all. If you work on the feeling of being: worthy, good, even wonderful, just as you are, without being dependent on what others think, this, in and of itself, could lead to physical and emotional health.

Today's treatment methods understand the connection between body and soul. Juvenal, a Roman poet who lived in the first century, and Maimonides in the eleventh century, spoke of this connection, with Maimonides equating between a healthy soul and a healthy body.

In my second book, I explain what happens if an illness has already developed (although I focus on depression, I think that all of this is true for other illnesses as well. In addition, I focus on the caregivers and not on the sick one, as they are an important factor in the illness of the sick one). His hardship can be alleviated using both the physical and the emotional insights I present there.

BIBLIOGRAPHY

Tal Asher, *Tafkido Shel Haben/bat zug shel hahole*, Facebook, 14 Jan 2021, https://www.facebook.com/photo/?fbid=10220226590869791&set=a.1426955228722 Accessed 20 Jan. 2021.

Doki Cohen *An Equally Worthy Child* (Israel: Focus Publishing, 2018)

William Styron, *Darkness Visible: A Memoir of Madness* (New York: Random, 1990)

Jamison Kay R. *An Unquiet Mind* (New York: Vintage Books, 1996)

Printed in Great Britain
by Amazon